This

How to Invest

for Beginners book

belongs to

Special Acknowledgment

To Adewunmi Gbogboade

Author of

"The Wealthy Home"

We thank you and greatly appreciate you for provoking us to good works!

Published by Kingdom Khai, LLC.
www.KingdomKhai.com

Table of Contents

WELCOME

Welcome to How to Invest for Beginners!

In this book you will learn the basics about investing from a beginner's perspective.

This resource will help you gain confidence as you dive into the world of investing, in a simple yet rewarding way.

We will talk about money, why you should invest, learn key investment terms and so much more!

Let's get started...

About the Authors

This workbook was written by a husband-and-wife team with a diverse professional background. While we are not "experts" in the investment world, we are students of investing.

We are experienced in accounting, business management, real estate and currently run our own small business and investment club.

We wrote this book for true beginners who want to learn more about investing in an easy way. This will help you become confident and start your journey on the road to generational wealth!

Chapter 1

Money Talks

Chapter 1: Money Talks

Talking about money can be a touchy subject, but there is one thing we can all agree upon, money is a part of our lives and having it or not having it can make a difference.

It is also an important key ingredient in the world of investing. One common misconception is that you must have a lot of "money" to start investing and that is simply not true, as you will learn.

As you gain competence you will gain confidence. Learning about investing will help you to be equipped to dive deeper. As you grow in your knowledge, understanding and experience, this will bring forth wisdom.

Matthew 6:33
But seek ye first the kingdom of God, and his righteousness; and all these things shall be added unto you.

Scripture

Ecclesiastes 5:10
Whoever loves money never has enough; whoever loves wealth is never satisfied with their income. This too is meaningless.

Scripture

Disclaimer: We encourage learning and growth through education. Keeping in perspective that we should all seek the guidance and provision of Our Creator. This tool is meant to empower you to be a good steward of the talents that the Most High gives you to manage. All information shared is for informational and entertainment purposes only. We do not proclaim to be experts, so invest at your own risk.

Chapter 1: Money Talks

Fact: Money in the bible was not what we know as our currency today! Gold is mentioned 417 times in the bible and silver 320 times. On top of that, the word "Money" is used 140 times, but there is a catch.

If you translate those occurrences of the word money into Hebrew, you will find that the word *kesep̄,* which is silver. So, one of the most common forms of monetary exchange in the bible was silver.

Fact: The first coins were minted (made) around 2,500 years ago. Paper money was first used in China over 1,000 years ago. The benefit of metal coins is that they are portable and durable.

The original value of a British pound was equal to a pound (in weight) of silver.

- Money is used to pay for various goods and services.
- It is also used to measure and store value.
- Money usually takes the form of coins, banknotes and bank balances.

Credit cards were first used in the United States in the 1920's.

Fact: It costs more money to make pennies and nickels than they're actually worth!

It costs the U.S. Mint about 2.10 cents to produce one penny and about 8.52 cents to make one nickel. This is primarily due to the price of copper and nickel — which have both gotten more expensive over time.

Fact: Coins stay in circulation for about 30 years before they get melted down and repurposed.

After about 30 years, coins become too worn down and tarnished to stay in circulation. So, the Federal Reserve melts them down and repurposes them.

Chapter 1: Money Talks

Fact: Did you know that two separate agencies create coins and paper money!
When you think of creating money, your mind may go straight to the U.S. Mint. But in reality, the U.S. Mint only makes coins (think pennies, nickels, dimes, and quarters). The Bureau of Engraving and Printing (BEP) is the agency that makes paper money.

Fact: There is no such thing as "paper" money.
Federal Reserve notes are actually made of 25% linen and 75% cotton, not paper!

Fact: Most U.S. currency isn't even in the U.S.
According to authorities, between one-half and two-thirds of the value of all U.S. currency in circulation is *outside* the United States. This is mostly because the U.S. dollar is the world's primary reserve currency.
So as a result, several nations use it for international trade and cash reserves.

Fact: There used to be a $100,000 bill!
This is one of our favorite fun facts about money! In 1934, the U.S. created a $100,000 bill, also known as a $100,000 Gold Certificate. While it's technically the largest banknote the government ever issued, it was never meant for public use.

Instead, Federal Reserve Bank branches used them for large inter-bank transactions. But still. Can you imagine what you'd do if you found a $100,000 bill on the sidewalk? Pause and think ☺

Reference for money facts:
https://www.clevergirlfinance.com/blog/money-facts/

ACTIVITY PAGE

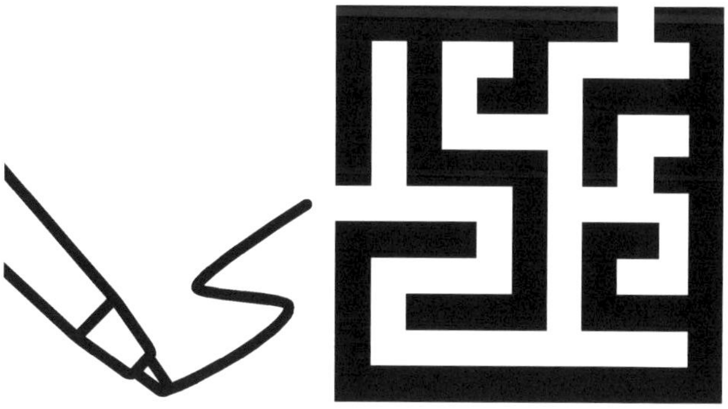

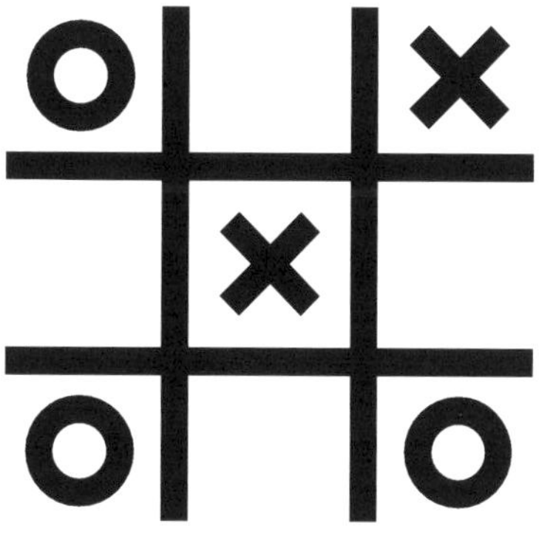

Chapter 1: Activity

So, to set a firm foundation, we must take a moment to ask a few questions.

Please be very honest with yourself to get the most of this learning process.

What does money mean to you?

What are some ways you can make money?

If you got a lot of money, how would you feel?

If you received a lump sum of money, how would you feel?

What would you do with your money?

Investors Notes

Chapter 2

Introduction to Investing:

What is Investing?

Chapter 2: What is Investing

Welcome to Investing!

Here is your introduction to the world of stocks, bonds, bulls, and bears. Before we jump to those topics, we must answer our most basic question. What is investing?

Investing is the act of allocating resources, usually money, with the expectation of generating an income or profit. (INVEST) In other words, investing is giving or paying money for something and expecting to make more money than you paid for it, at a later time. You invest your money to grow your money. If you invest in the right thing, you could grow your money by leaps and bounds.

The average yearly return or money you make on an investment, is 8-10%. Imagine if you could make $10 dollars on every $100 you have, or $100 dollars on every $1,000! That would be a 10% profit on your money.

I know that may sound good, but why invest?

Why should you invest?

One of the biggest reasons to invest is because it's wise (i.e., very smart) to prepare for the future. It also can lead to something called generational wealth. We'll touch on that in a bit. Investing your money in good investments, shows that you know how to handle and manage your wealth. In other words, it shows that you know what to do with your money. Let me ask you a question.

Have you ever seen or heard of a celebrity, or an athlete, making millions of dollars and then years later they're broke out on the street? The biggest reason that someone who makes a lot of money at one time and no longer has any money after a short period of time, is because they did not know what to do with their money.

Chapter 2: What is Investing

There's a saying that states "money is power", but it probably should be phrased "knowing what to do with your money is power". It doesn't do anyone any good to have money when they don't know what to do with it. This is a key to personal finance management, a.k.a. budgeting.

I can speak to this from experience. At one point in time, I witnessed firsthand a close family member blowing through over $80,000 dollars, a house and multiple vehicles that they inherited in less than a year! All these things were passed on from one generation to another. One generation worked hard to build up hundreds of thousands of dollars of transferable wealth over their lifetime and that next generation tore it down in a blink of an eye. This is not how it's supposed to be. This real-life example, like the celebrity example, depicts a picture of someone who didn't know what to do with their money.

What is generational wealth and how does investing lead to it?

A positive takeaway, from the personal example stated, is that one member of the family obtained enough wealth to give it to their next of kin after they had passed on. This helps us define "generational wealth".

Proverbs 13:22
"A good man leaves an inheritance to his children's children."

Scripture

Chapter 2: What is Investing

Proverbs 13:22 keeps our life goals, our vision and our legacy front and center when we're choosing how to use our money today. Generational wealth refers to resources passed on from one generation of a family to another, such as stocks, bonds, real estate, and family businesses. (INVEST) For example, $80,000 in cash plus possessions given from a parent to their child.

Have you ever heard of an inheritance?

Inheritance is the sum of items involved in the passing on of material property from one generation to another, usually within the family. This process can be seen in cases involving transfers from older parents (donors) to their adult children (heirs). (INVEST)

So, in summary, generational wealth ideally should be inherited. Investing typically plays a huge part in transferring wealth from one generation to the next. This is because, in many instances, the wealth being transferred to the next generation comes in the form and an investment account.

Now, you may not know anyone who has an “investment account” and be thinking “isn’t a savings account” good enough? Of, course! A savings account is definitely, a good thing .

However, please know that there is a huge difference between an investment account and a savings account.

Chapter 2: What is Investing

Savings vs Investing, there is a difference.

Matthew 25:14–30

14 "Again, it will be like a man going on a journey, who called his
servants and entrusted his wealth to them. 15 To one he gave five bags
of gold, to another two bags, and to another one bag, each according
to his ability. Then he went on his journey. 16 The man who had
received five bags of gold went at once and put his money to work and
gained five bags more. 17 So also, the one with two bags of gold gained
two more. 18 But the man who had received one bag went off, dug a
hole in the ground and hid his master's money.

Scripture

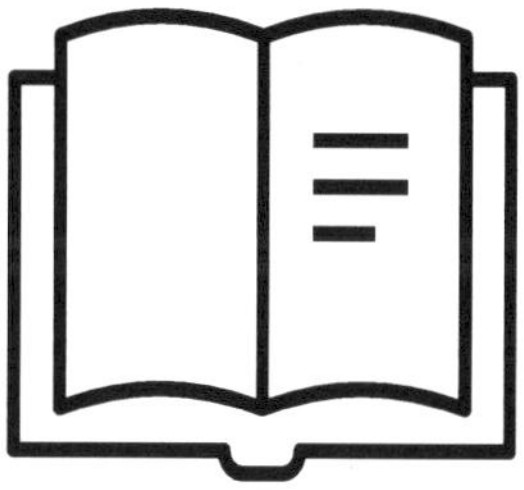

Here's some insight from this passage. The man who received one bag or talent, and dug a hole in the ground, saved his money. This would be holding the money, and not even putting it in a savings account. Resulting in zero gain.

The other two men put their money to work investing it. The result is that they gained money on top of the money they invested. Does this famed bible passage reflect modern day reality?

Chapter 2: What is Investing

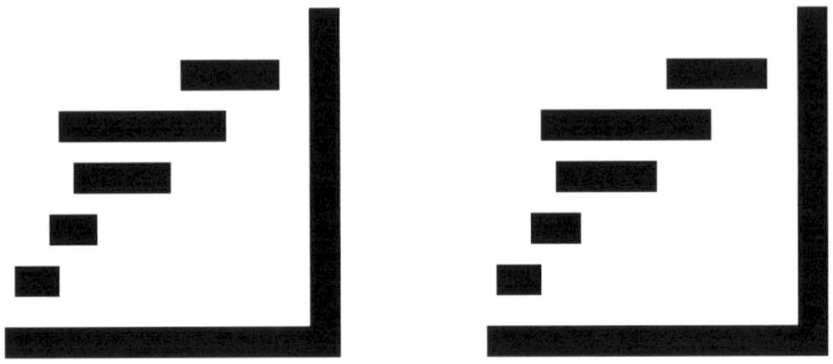

Well, in a savings account your money gains a national average of 0.07% yearly interest. That's not even 1%! However, we have already mentioned that the average market return on an investment is 8-10% per year.

So, if you were to inherit a savings account with $20,000 and did not take it out for a few years, your inheritance would likely stay around $20,000.

However, if it was an investment account with $20,000, then you would inherit upwards of $24,000 after the same timeframe. Now imagine if your inheritance of $20,000 was being invested over 10 or even 20 or more years. This is the beginning stages of building generational wealth.

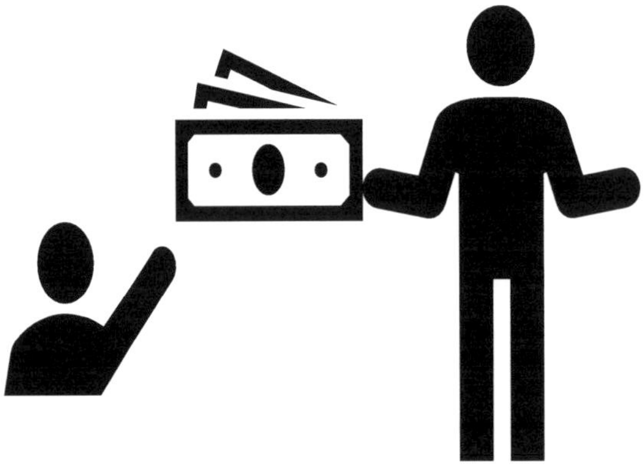

Investment Terms

A true intro to investing isn't complete without learning some investment lingo. So, here's a quick starter kit to help you start talking like a Wall Street regular.

Stock Market

The stock market refers to the collection of markets and exchanges where regular activities of buying, selling, and issuance of shares of publicly held companies take place.

Portfolio

A portfolio is a collection of financial investments like stocks, bonds, commodities,

Market Index

A stock market index is an index or guide that measures a stock market, or a subset of the stock market, that helps investors compare current price levels with past prices to calculate market performance.

S&P 500

The S&P 500 measures the value of the stocks of the 500 largest corporations by market capitalization listed on the New York Stock Exchange or Nasdaq Composite. The intention of Standard & Poor's is to have a price that provides a quick look at the stock market and economy.

These are just a few terms courtesy of Investopedia.com (INVEST) to get you started, be sure to go through the list of terms located in the glossary in order to increase your investment vocabulary and wisdom.

Stock Market History

In this section we'll do a very brief outline of Stock Market History.

People have been trading and or bartering with each other all throughout civilization, however, here are just a few notable recorded dates.

- In the 1300s, Europe's Venetian lenders were the first to start trading securities from other governments.
- In 1773 big business in England, led to a formal stock exchange in London.
- In 1817 in the US colonies, "The New York Stock Exchange" was formed.
- In 1971 NASDAQ came along to challenge The New York Stock exchange with the ability to trade securities electronically. (ORJ)

That was just a bit of market history regarding documented market infancy and growth. It's worth mentioning that today , "The New York Stock Exchange" is regarded as the largest and perhaps most powerful market of them all. Now, the markets longevity has not come without challenges. It's highly important that a good investor, (which you will become), obtain a solid understanding of these challenges.

Crashes and Recoveries

Historically, the stock markets have crashed or lost lots of money due to a rapid and often unanticipated drop in stock prices. So, here's a few examples we may remember. (ORJ)

- "Black Tuesday" in 1929, which gave way to "The Great Depression".
- Then we have "The .Com Bubble" in 2000.
- "The Mortgage Crisis of 2008 and the "The P Word of 2020".

These are just a few notable market crashes. However, the markets have always recovered or went back up after overcoming the challenges associated with these crashes. In order to become the excellent investor, you're soon to be, it's important to have a strong grip on this area.

Understanding Crashes and Recoveries

Why is this important to understand crashes and recoveries? If we understand the history and nature of market crashes and recoveries, we'll be more confident and emotionally stable when investing. Keeping the history of market crashes in mind, they still average an 8-10% annual return. (ORJ) This means that the markets may sometime "yo-yo" or "roller coaster" up and down and up and down. It could make you a little sick if you're not prepared to handle it. One way to look at this crucial point is by acknowledging the two states of the market.

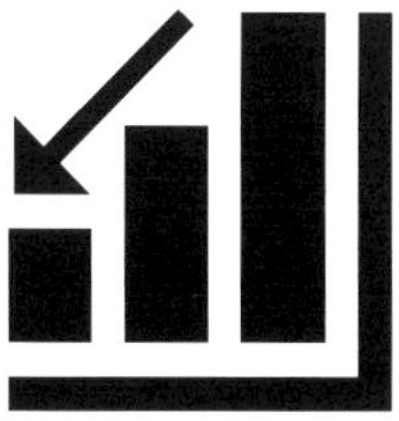

Two States of the Market
Bears vs Bulls

Market crashes and recoveries give way to the two main states of the market. The first is called a “bull market”. When stock prices are up, this is known as a “bull” market. The other state is called a “bear market”. When stock prices are down, this is known as our “bear” market.

Buy low, sell High.
Ever heard that one before?

The perfect time to buy stock, is when the bear market prices are low. This is like your stock being on sale! When the sale is over, and the stock price has risen, you can sell the stock at the higher price and profit the difference. That’s good investing and shows a thorough understanding of the market.

$

ACTIVITY PAGE

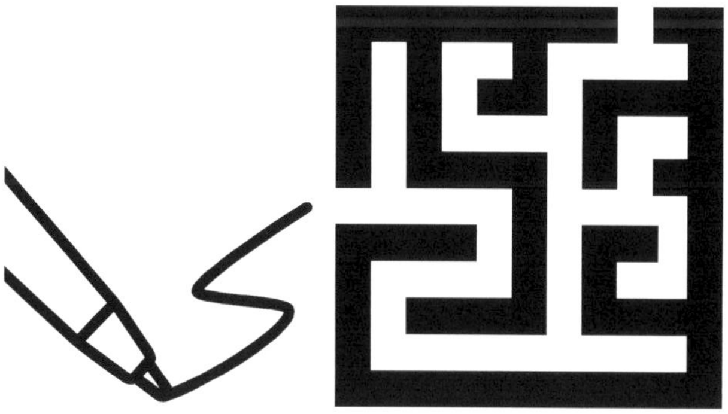

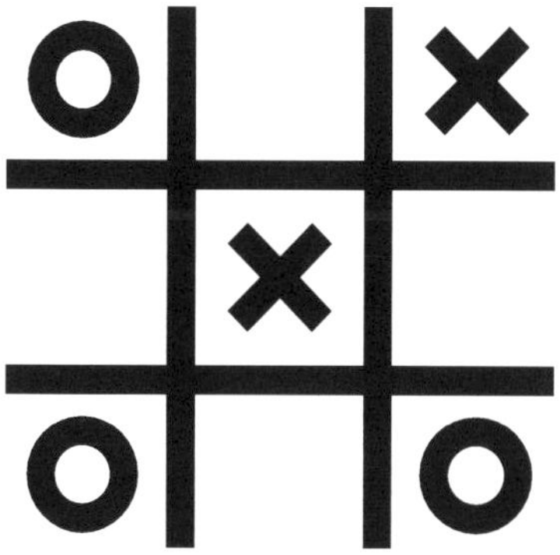

Chapter 2: Activity

Define the following terms using the definitions in the glossary.

Capital

____

____

Security

____

____

Dollar-cost averaging

____

____

Stockbroker

____

____

Bond

____

____

Traditional IRA

____

____

ETF

____

____

Investors Notes

Investors Notes

Investors Notes

Chapter 3

The Making of an Investor: Setting Up for Success

Chapter 3: The Making of an Investor: Setting up for Success

Now we will take a shift and explore something that may often get overlooked and that is MINDSET.

A positive mindset can make all the difference because accomplishing anything valuable with a bad attitude is almost impossible. So, if we have a negative state of mind, how can we learn the things we need to know in order to gain knowledge and understanding to accomplish our goals?

The following quote, from Brain Coach Jim Kwik, sums it up:

"All learning is state dependent" ~Jim Kwik

What this tells us is that a positive state of mind enhances our opportunity to learn. So, as we build our knowledge banks, we want to be able to recognize the various states of mind that can derail our efforts toward success. Let's dive in....

What are the types of mindsets?

The following are some of the most common mind states that an individual may find themselves in:

- **Anxious mind state:** It's about the future, the what ifs, disasters, and butterflies in the stomach

- **Depressed mind state:** If anxiety is about the future, depression is often about the past—mistakes, regrets, roads not taken.

- **Fearful mind state:** We walk on eggshells and get good at appeasing others and avoiding confrontation. This could be linked to triggers that open childhood wounds.

- **Pessimistic mind state:** In this state of mind, you often focus on what is negative and what could possibly go wrong in a situation. Also, a pessimist may question the validity of optimistic results. (PsychologyToday)

So, you may be saying, "Yea, I hear it all the time, be positive, think happy thoughts, blah, blah."

I can think of a state of mind that might describe that kind of thinking, I'm just saying. ☺

Your mindset or state of mind is critical when it comes to investing, because it will be what helps you create your "Investment Philosophy".

"Your investment philosophy should capture the beliefs and principles that will guide how you invest." (ORJ)

A positive mindset makes all the difference

Positive thinking, or an optimistic attitude, is the practice of focusing on the good in any given situation. It can have a big impact on your physical and mental health. That doesn't mean you ignore reality or deny the existence of problems. It simply means you approach the good and the bad in life with the expectation that things will go well. (WEBMD)

Romans 8:28
All things work together for good to them that love God, to them who are the called according to his purpose.

Scripture

Philippians 4:8
Finally, brethren, whatsoever things are true, whatsoever things are honest, whatsoever things are just, whatsoever things are pure, whatsoever things are lovely, whatsoever things are of good report; if there be any virtue, and if there be any praise, think on these things

Scripture

Chapter 3: The Making of an Investor: Setting up for Success

Personal finances: What about your house?

Now that we have taken care of our mind, we must look at our House. You may be surprised to know that taking care of your household finances is linked to economics! How so, well if we dig into the word economics for its scriptural basis, we will find that it is linked to managing the house a.k.a. stewardship.

Once we have a positive mind state, we need to evaluate our house stewardship. This will boil down to how you are managing your house finances. Do you have a system in place aka a budget?

If not, don't worry in the next chapter we will go over various budget methods that you can use to get your systems up and running.

Audit your finances

In the meantime, we need to audit our budget (or spending habits if you don't have a budget just yet).

You might wonder, "Is budgeting even in the bible?" I am glad you asked, and I am happy to say it most certainly is.

Luke 14:28-30

28 If you wanted to build a tower, you would first sit down and decide how much it would cost. You must see if you have enough money to finish the job. 29 If you don't do that, you might begin the work, but you would not be able to finish. And if you could not finish it, then all who would see it would laugh at you. 30 They would say, 'This man began to build but was not able to finish!'

Scripture

It is very important to make a plan and follow it the best we can to achieve our future goals, whether that is generational wealth, retirement, a vacation, a new home or all of the above.

Chapter 3: The Making of an Investor: Setting up for Success

What is this audit and how do you do it?

When you perform an audit, you are inspecting all your accounts by performing a thorough review and documenting your findings.

The findings of this audit will reveal so many things about where you are. Here are some things that could be uncovered:

It will let us know if you have a "fake budget".

This is a term coined by me and means, you have a pretty budget that has amounts and is broken down and everything, it is perfect! However, the problem is, it is nothing like what you really do with your money on a monthly basis. If you compare what is on the fake budget to what you bring in and spend, they are night and day.

It can be a huge challenge to admit if you indeed are operating a fake budget, but it is very important to be honest in your audit. This will allow you to set up for success, as you move to investor status! Also, keep in mind, that once you do your audit, it will also reveal where your priorities are.

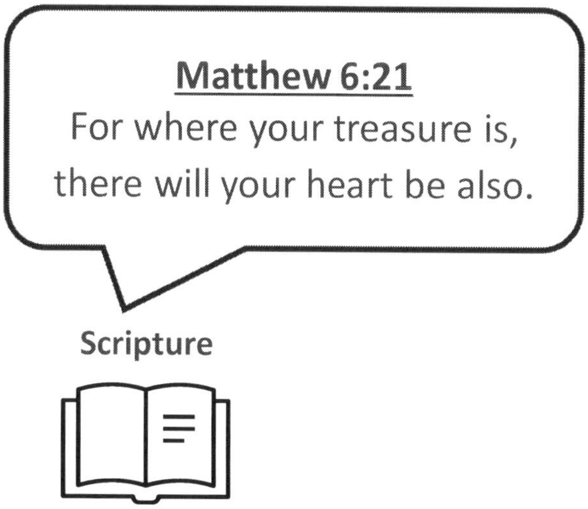

Chapter 3: The Making of an Investor: Setting up for Success

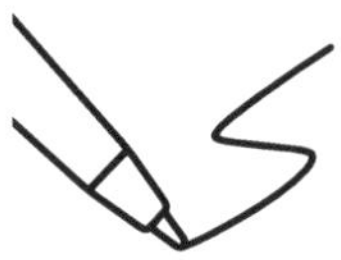

Things to consider during your audit

Here are some things to consider when performing your audit:

1. Look at every dollar you spend (every expense), no matter what it's for. Write it down.

    - Mindful moment: If you had to turn over EVERY receipt for every purchase, expense, and/or disbursement that you've made for the past 90 days, to be compiled and shared with 10 people you know, are there things that this would show that you may not be comfortable with people knowing you do, consume or participate in?
    - Are there things you would not want people to, see? Of course, we have private things that you may not want everybody all in your business, but are there things that you know should not be there?
    - Have you ever considered how your budget could reveal some of your deepest, darkest secrets?

2. Moving on, what are all your streams of income, even if it's just $50 dollars a month? Write it down and account for it.

    - When you compare what you spend to what you bring in, is there a deficit or a surplus?
    - Can you account for every dollar, or are there some missing pieces, or unknown expenditures?
    - Do you see any spending habits that you did not realize you had?

Chapter 3: The Making of an Investor: Setting up for Success

Here are some more tips to keep in mind as you audit, create, or redefine your budget:

- Commit---Having a budget is a relationship. You must be loyal, committed and diligent. If you cheat on your budget, you are mishandling your talents.
- Budgets are for everyone----- of all income levels. You can budget $1. Don't make the mistake of thinking you have to have a certain amount of money to have a budget.
- Be Honest-----Honesty is Key! You are only cheating yourself if you are not upfront with where your finances are flowing to.

Once you have completed your budget audit or just an examination of your personal finances, the next order of business is to look at your emotions and your risk tolerance.

What about Emotions?

When evaluating your emotions and what type of investor you would be, according to Our Rich Journey, there are 4 types of investors to look at when considering your position:

The Safe Investor. An investor that focuses on safety typically values principal balance preservation overgrowth. This type of investor prefers an investment that can outperform the rate of inflation. At the same time, this investor has little to no interest in investing money in an asset that could potentially reduce their principal balance invested. For this investor, the potential reward is generally not worth the risk. This type of investor would prefer to place their investments in certificates of deposit (CDs), money markets, or U.S. Treasuries.

Chapter 3: The Making of an Investor: Setting up for Success

The Income Investor. This investor's objective is to build a portfolio that produces beyond just capital gains. With an income focused portfolio, the objective would be to generate a fixed level of income from the investment portfolio each month. An investor focused on income may opt to allocate his/her portfolio more heavily into high yielding dividend investments like blue chip stocks and REITs. (See glossary of terms) (ORJ)

The Growth Investor. An investor that focuses on growth typically focuses on companies that the investor believes will grow at a rate that beats the overall stock market. A growth focused portfolio focuses on investments that will produce significant capital gains. This type of investor understands the higher risk associated with focusing primarily on growth in his/her portfolio. At the same time, this type of investor is willing to take the risk in exchange for a potentially greater reward in the form of greater portfolio growth. This type of investor will build a portfolio more heavily into low cap companies, newer companies that are expected to make significant impacts to everyday life, and/or ETFs that hold a disproportionately high percentage of low cap companies, new and innovative companies, or technology companies that tend to offer greater potential growth. (ORJ)

The Stable Investor. An investor that focuses on stability typically wants to see portfolio growth, however they want to avoid significant risks. With a stability focused portfolio, the investor understands that all market investments involve some level of risk. The investor's objective is to create a portfolio that produces the most stable portfolio returns possible year-to-year. An investor focused on stability may allocate his/her portfolio more heavily into index funds and ETFs designed to track benchmark indices. (ORJ)

Chapter 3: The Making of an Investor: Setting up for Success

Establishing your Risk Tolerance

Now that we have talked about the different types of investors, let's discuss the idea of risk tolerance.

Your risk tolerance is your level of comfort with the ups and downs of investing in the stock market. It's unique to each individual. (ORJ)

Determining your risk tolerance will help you select the best investments for you as an individual. It is extremely important to find investments that match your risk tolerance, otherwise you run the risk of causing undo stress upon yourself, because the volatility of the investments may cause you panic or worry. (ORJ)

What are the different levels of risk tolerance?

<u>Low Risk Tolerance:</u> Investors with low risk tolerance understand the need to grow their money faster than the rate of inflation. At the same time, a low risk tolerance investor is typically conservative and primarily concerned with the risk of losing large portions of his/her portfolio. A low risk tolerance investor may view investing in the market as stressful. Constant fluctuations in the market may have the low risk tolerance investor repeatedly worried about the performance of his/her portfolio, whether the investor will be able to achieve his/her short-term goals, whether the investor will be able to retire, or pay for a big purchase. Investments that match this risk tolerance profile typically include a higher allocation in basic savings accounts, money market funds, and certificates of deposit. (ORJ)

Medium Risk Tolerance: Investors with medium risk tolerance tend to invest in a balanced mix of stocks and bonds for average returns with average risk. They typically aren't too concerned by short duration declines in the market or small dips in the value of their portfolio. However, if the stock market declines over a long period of time or if the investor's portfolio drops significantly by a large percentage in a very short period, the medium risk tolerance investor may become stressed or anxious. Investors with this level of tolerance are prone to panic selling if declines are for a sustained period. Investors at this level tend to have mid-term investment goals, such as retirement within 5 to 10 years. Investments that match this risk tolerance profile typically include a combination of stock and bond index funds and sector ETFs. (ORJ)

High Risk Tolerance: Investors with high risk tolerance tend to invest aggressively for maximum returns with maximum risk. At the same time, these investors understand and accept the higher level of risk associated with aggressive investing. High risk tolerance investors typically aren't bothered by the daily ups and downs of their investment. Instead, they are focused on the long-term growth of their portfolio. Consequently, high risk tolerance investors tend to pick investments that support long-term goals because their investments have more time to potentially recover from drops in value. Investments that match this risk tolerance profile may include some individual stocks and an investment portfolio that typically consists of a very high allocation of stocks compared to bonds (e.g., more than 90% stocks), with some high-risk tolerance investors omit bonds from their portfolios entirely. (ORJ)

Chapter 3: The Making of an Investor: Setting up for Success

Paper losses vs Actual losses

Paper profits and losses are the same as unrealized gains and unrealized losses. The profit only exists in the investor's ledger in other words on paper. The loss or gain does not become an actual or realized loss or gain until the asset, i.e., investment is closed out and settled in real money. (INVEST)

Let's take an example, so if you check the balance of your brokerage account and it shows that you have a loss of -$10 or a gain of +$10, if you decide to sell the investment that is causing the gain or loss, then you would have an actual or realized gain or loss. If you just see it and leave it, it is just on paper and is not realized.

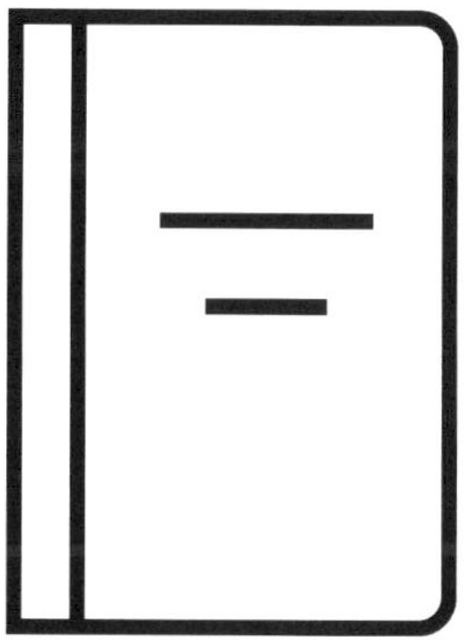

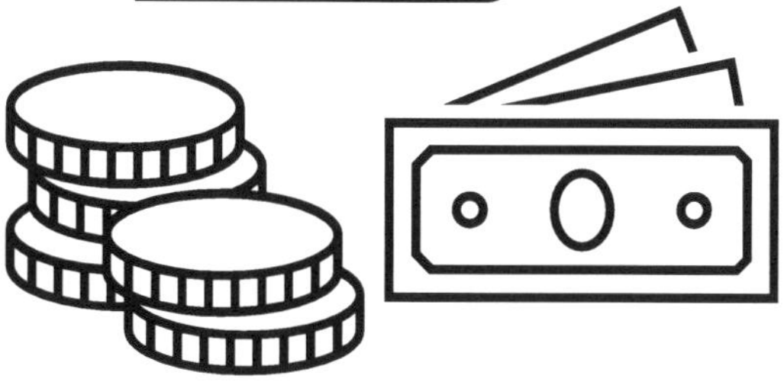

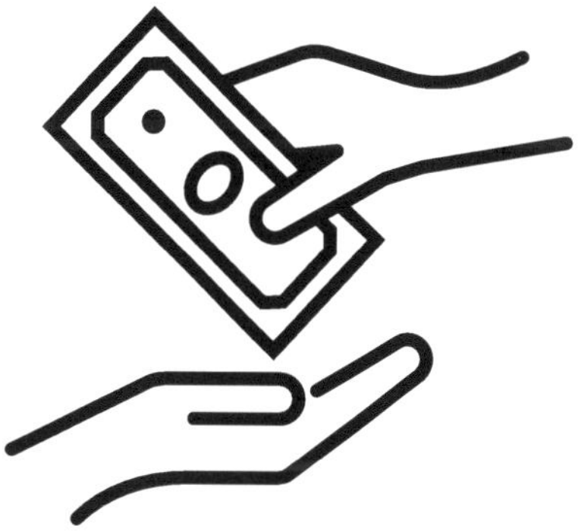

Activity Page

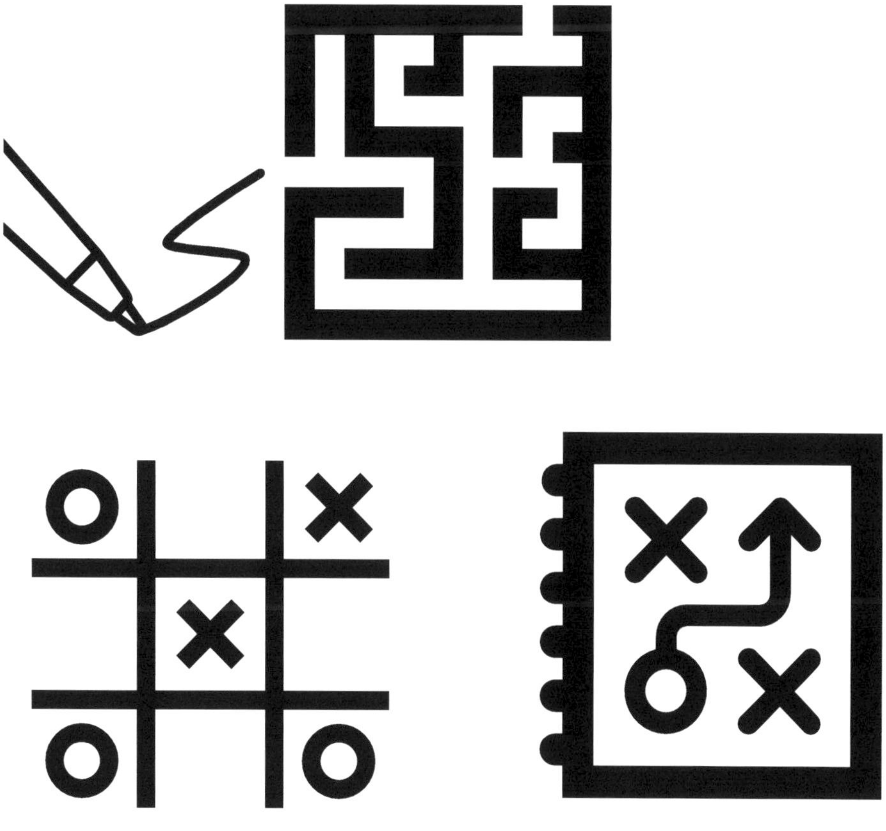

CHAPTER 3: ACTIVITY

Affirmations for a Positive Mindset

Repeat the below affirmations each morning for at least 30 days and then document how you feel after doing the process. Use the tracking sheet to help keep you motivated. The following are based on the indicated bible verse.

- **I am a beloved child of the Most High Creator.** *(Jeremiah 31:3)*
- **I am held in my Father's hand and need not fear.** *(John 10:28-29)*
- **I am worthy of love because God loves me.** *(Ephesians 2:4-5)*
- **I am treasured by the Father.** *(Deuteronomy 14:2)*
- **I am God's masterpiece.** *(Ephesians 2:10)*
- **I am chosen and appointed by God.** *(John 15:16)*
- **I am healed from sin by God's love.** *(1 Peter 2:24)*
- **I am abundant.** *(2 Corinthians 12:9)*
- **I am fearfully and wonderfully made.** *(Psalm 139:14)*
- **I am brave.** *(Psalm 23:4)*
- **I am made in the image of God.** *(Genesis 1:27)*
- **I am free.** *(Galatians 5:1)*
- **I am redeemed through the Messiah.** *(Ephesians 1:7)*
- **I am triumphant.** *(1 John 5:4)*
- **I am gifted.** *(1 Peter 4:10)*

Date	Affirmation completed	Date	Affirmation completed	Date	Affirmation completed

Date	Affirmation completed	Date	Affirmation completed
		Date	Bonus

Investors Notes

Chapter 4

It's all about Systems!

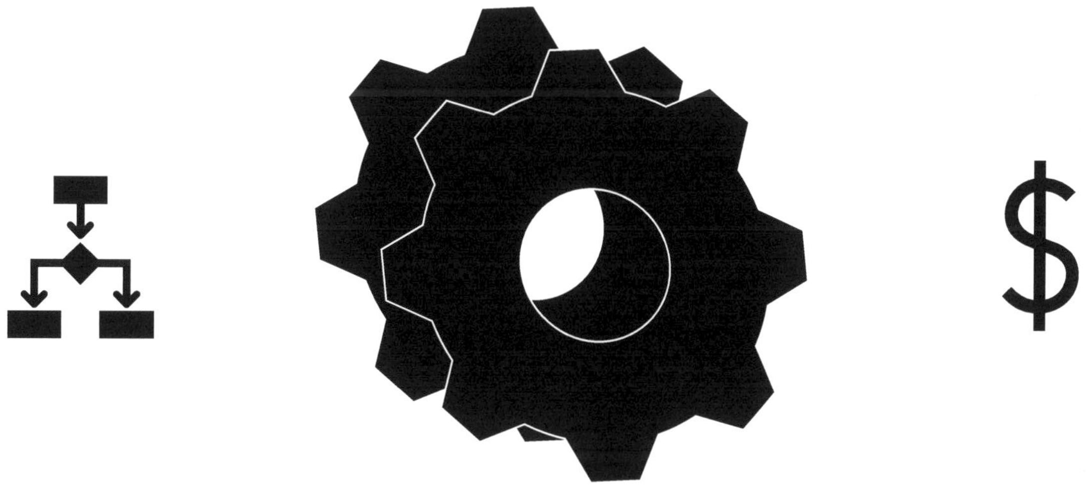

Chapter 4: It's all about systems

As we jump into systems, let's first define the word "System"

"A system is a collection of elements or components that are organized for a common purpose."(TECH)

On your investing journey you want to position for success, and one important element is to have systems in place to help you achieve your goals. As we discussed in Chapter 3, one of the most important elements of your system is your BUDGET!

Budget: "an estimate of income and expenses for a set period of time". (MONEY254)

For some this may be a term that makes them cringe and want to go hide their head under a pillow, but to be honest, a budget is money's BFF (best friend forever). They make a great team and complement each other very well.

Let's start with exploring the most common types of budgets, just to gain some understanding that there are different approaches you could use. Who doesn't like variety???

Note: Some of these will seem like they only apply to businesses, however the concepts can also be used when organizing your personal finances.

Budget Type #1: Incremental

Incremental budgeting takes last year's actual figures and adds or subtracts a percentage to obtain the current year's budget. Then you would add in any new expenses that you expect to have for the year.

Budget Type #2: Value Proposition

In value proposition budgeting, you would consider what value any item on your budget is generating to justify it still being considered a part of your budget. (CORP)

For example: Cable TV Expense. If you are considering this item in your value proposition, when updating your budget, you would ask yourself,

1. Does having Cable TV create value for my family and I?
2. Does the value of the item outweigh its cost? If not, then is there another reason why the cost is justified?

<u>Budget Type #3: Zero-based.</u>

In a zero-based budget, you start from scratch every year. Instead of building on previous budgets, you assess your current situation and decide which expenses will be worth keeping and which ones should go. (CORP)

<u>Budget Type #4 The 50/30/10/10 rule</u>

The 50/30/10/10 budgeting method is easy to set up and most find it easy to sustain over time. In this type of budgeting system,

- 50% of your income goes toward necessities such as housing, utilities, and transportation.
- 30% of your income goes toward more discretionary type items, such as personal care wants such as elaborate clothing and entertainment costs such as going out to eat or going to movies.
- 10% of income should be set aside for savings - and this can include retirement savings
- 10% of income set aside for your emergency funds for things like car repairs or medical bills.

<u>Budget Type #5 The Reverse Budget</u>

The <u>reverse budget</u> focuses on savings. Instead of starting your month with how much you can spend, you first figure out how much money you want to set aside for savings and then use the rest to meet your expenses. (CORP)

Budget Type #6 Debt Avalanche Budget

The debt avalanche method allows you to pay off your debts in order of their interest rate, from highest to lowest. This technique is specifically advantageous for someone with more than one debt and wants to get out of debt quickly and in the most cost-efficient way possible. (CORP)

Budget Type #7 The 60% Solution Budget

The 60% solution is also known as the 60/40 budgeting method. This is a good choice, especially if you're just starting with budgeting. It's also recommended if you are trying to get your finances under control and don't have any credit card debt or other financial obligations that need to be paid off right away.

With this method your "committed expenses" that is, necessities, plus nonessentials you've committed to — are within 60% of your income. The other 40 is broken up into 10% increments and here are some examples:

- 10% to retirement savings in your 401(k) or IRA.
- 10% to long-term savings in a taxable investment account, meaning you can access the money within three days, but not unless you need to. The money will sit and compound (more on that later). It includes your emergency fund for things like medical bills and savings for planned purchases like cars.

- 10% to short-term savings in a high-yield savings account that you can instantly access or use to transfer money to your checking account via the web. This is for more frequent, unplanned needs like repairs, as well as vacations and holiday gifts.
- 10% to fun money that you can spend on anything as long as it doesn't exceed 10% of your income. (CORP)

Budget Type #8 The Envelop Method Budget

The envelope method is a budgeting strategy that's all about splitting up your money into different envelopes. You use each envelope to designate where the money in it should go. Give the envelope a category and write it on the front of the envelope. You can only spend the money in that envelope on that expense. (RAMSEY)

Note: This method is designed for people who primarily spend in cash.

Now that we have discussed all kinds of budget methods, you will have to decide what would work for you and your situation. Just putting a simple budget in place can help catapult you in organization and positioning by simply knowing where your money is coming from and most importantly knowing where it is going to. Run the numbers and see what you come up with.

We recommend getting a budget planner, especially if you like seeing things written down. See the Reference page for more details on our recommendations.

ACTIVITY PAGE

Sample Budget

Below is a sample budget to help you get started if you don't have one or if you want to start something new.

SAMPLE BUDGET PLANNER

BUDGET MONTH

SOURCE OF INCOME

Source	Actual	Difference
Total		

BUDGET REVIEW TOTALS

Category	Actual	Difference
Income		
Recurring Expenses		
Other Expenses		
Debt		
Savings		
Investment		
Total		

RECURRING EXPENSES

Expense	Actual	Difference

SAVINGS

Category	Actual	Difference

INVESTMENT

Category	Actual	Difference

INVESTORS NOTES

Chapter 5

What is a good company?

CHAPTER 5: WHAT IS A GOOD COMPANY

What is a good company

What is a good company to invest in? How can you tell? These two questions should be answered after first understanding the positions involved in the process of lending. You are looking to find a good company to lend to and they are looking to borrow from you.
Let's examine these next definitions.

- <u>A lender</u>

is an individual, a public or private group, or a financial institution that makes funds available to a person or business with the expectation that the funds will be repaid. Repayment will include the payment of any interest or fees. *(INVEST)*

- <u>A debtor</u>

is a company or individual who owes money. If the debt is in the form of a loan from a financial institution, the debtor is referred to as a borrower, and if the debt is in the form of securities—such as bonds—the debtor is referred to as an issuer. *(INVEST)*

<u>Prov. 22:7</u>
The rich rule over the poor and the borrower is slave to the lender.

Scripture

CHAPTER 5: WHAT IS A GOOD COMPANY

There are two positions, one is subject to the other. However, there's some vital elements that both sides need to have, in order for all parties to reach their goals.

➢ Credit

The ability to borrow money or access goods or services with the understanding that you'll pay later. (WEBSTER)

➢ Credibility

The level of which your credit is measured. (WEBSTER)

Let's simplify these terms a bit. Credit is the maximum amount of something entrusted to you, based on how much you can be trusted, a.k.a. your credibility. Do you have a trustworthy reputation? Does the company you will lend to have a trustworthy reputation?

When picking a good company, the better the credit and credibility are, the better chance for success. This is the foundational thought process you want to have as you build the actual tool that will lead you to picking the right company and or stock. It should put you in the mood to develop your criteria checklist.

Chapter 5: What is a good company

Develop a Set of Criteria

Now it is time to develop a set of criteria aka a checklist! You need to have a pinpoint set of measurables to make it easy for you to say yay or nay, to any stock or company you consider investing in. List out specific things to look at. This will become your measuring tool. Here are some examples.

- Leadership
- Share Price
- Dividend Payout
- Profit Margin
- Volume
- History
- Moat

Activity Page

Chapter 5: Activity

Begin writing down your criteria for your checklist. Think about what measurables are important to you and use the examples stated to prompt you.

¢

- Share Price
- Dividend Payout
- Profit Margin

Investors Notes

Chapter 6

What are Financials?

Chapter 6: What are financials?

When you are looking to start investing, you will quickly learn that it is important to know exactly what you are looking at when you start to look at the financial statements of a company or business. These handy documents will give you a glimpse into how the company is doing and how they've faired historically.

What is the SEC Form 10-Q anyway?

The SEC Form 10-Q is an all-inclusive earnings report of financial performance that must be submitted quarterly by all public companies to the Securities and Exchange Commission (SEC) (Investopedia). In the 10-Q, corporations are required to disclose pertinent information regarding their finances as a result of their business operations.

A 10-Q must be filed for each of the first three quarters of the company's fiscal year. As an investors you can use the earnings report to gauge how well a company is run and whether the company is doing well.

Now let's look at some key factors related to an Earnings Report:

- The 10-Q must be filed 40 or 45 days after the end of their quarter, depending on the size.
- The form 10-Q provides investors with information they can compare to previous periods and use to evaluate the outlook for the stock's performance.
- Keep in mind the Form 10-Q is not an audited statement, unlike the annual Form 10-K companies are also required to file. (INVEST)

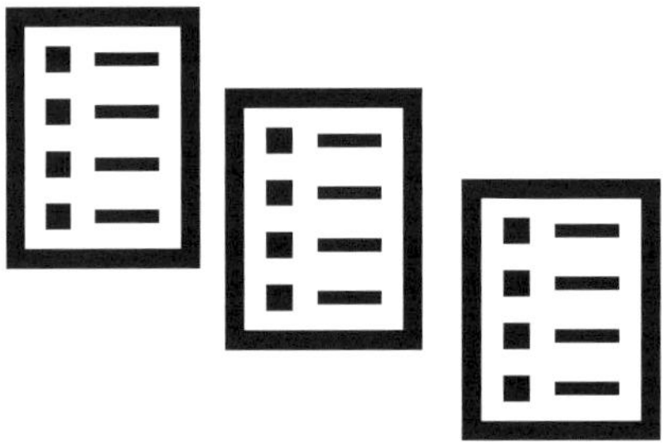

Chapter 6: What are financials?

What Is the Difference Between a 10-K and a 10-Q?

The main difference between Forms 10-K and 10-Q lies in the frequency and the amount of info they contain. Form 10-K is an annual report, filed at the end of a company's fiscal year. It summarizes all the data for the year, including the fourth quarter. In contrast, Form 10-Q is filed three times a year, at the end of a company's fiscal quarter. It details financial info for that quarter. (INVEST)

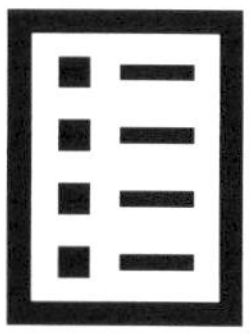

What are the main sections of the 10-Q?

The following is a listing of the main components of the 10-Q:

- **Income Statement**

  The income statement primarily focuses on a company's revenues and expenses during a particular period. Once expenses are subtracted from revenues, the statement produces a company's profit figure called net income.

- **Balance Sheet**

  The balance sheet provides an overview of assets, liabilities, and shareholders' equity as a snapshot in time.

- **Statement of Cash Flows**

  The cash flow statement measures how well a company generates cash to pay its debt obligations, fund its operating expenses, and fund investments.

- **Statement of Retained Earnings**

  The statement of changes in equity records how profits are retained within a company for future growth or distributed to external parties.

➢ **Management's discussion and disclosures**

Management discussion and analysis (MD&A) is a section within a company's annual report or quarterly filing where executives analyze the company's performance. This section can also include a discussion of compliance, risks, and future plans, such as goals and new projects.

In addition to analyzing the financial statements, it's important to analyze any financial risks, such as litigation, that could pose a threat to a company.

<u>How to analyze a 10-Q?</u>

Here are some general steps to take when evaluating a 10-Q:

- How did the company perform over the last quarter?
- How did the performance compare to the previous quarter, or to the same quarter in previous years?
- Have revenues improved or taken a hit on a quarter-to-quarter basis?
- Is the cost of sales increasing, meaning that it is more expensive to bring in revenue?

Something to keep in mind, is that the periods right before and after the quarterly report is released are essential times to pay attention to a corporation's stock price. Depending on whether or not a company meets its earnings goals, the stock price will see a sharp increase or decrease in its price.

% CHAPTER 6: WHAT ARE FINANCIALS?

What are financial Ratios and why are they important?

Now that we have tackled the 10-Q and some of its parts, next let's touch just a tiny bit on financial ratios.

In simple words, a financial ratio is a matter of dividing to get a percentage, in other words taking one number from a business's financial statements and dividing it by another. The resulting answer gives you a measure that you can use to compare to evaluate investment prospects.

Financial ratios can offer insight into different aspects of a company's financial health, from how it can cover its debt to how it utilizes its assets. As you become more advanced in your analysis of companies, these ratios will become very useful in assessing your next potential investment.

Now we will explore just a couple ratios to get a feel for the various types that are out there.

Profitability ratios %

- **Net profit margin = After tax net profit / Net sales**

This ratio illustrations the net income generated by each dollar of sales. It measures the percentage of sales revenue retained by the company after operating expenses, interest and taxes have been paid. (INVEST)

- **Return on shareholders' equity = Net income / Shareholders' equity**

This ratio indicates the amount of after-tax profit generated for each dollar of equity. A measure of the rate of return the shareholders received on their investment. (INVEST)

Activity Page

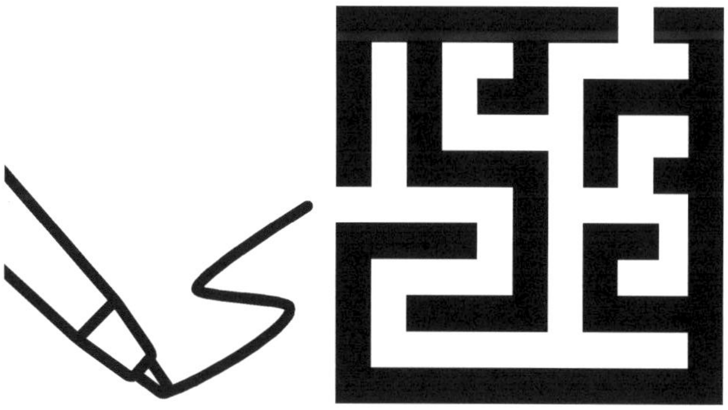

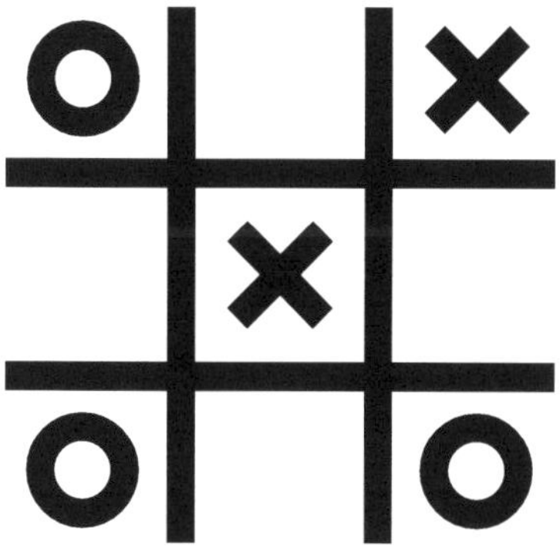

Chapter 6: Activity

Financial Ratios: Define the following ratios

Leverage ratios

Debt-to-equity ratio = Total liabilities / Shareholders' equity

Debt-to-asset ratio = Total liabilities / Total assets

Liquidity ratios

Working capital ratio = Current assets / Current liabilities

Cash ratio = Liquid assets / Current liabilities

Chapter 6: Sample Financial Statements

The following are 3 sample financial statements for your review to get a feel for what they look like and what would be contained in each type of statement.

Income Statement	(all numbers in $000)		Good to know Tips!!
Revenue	Year to Date Amount		
Gross sales		X	Income statements will should have the following sections: Revenue, Cost of Sales (or Cost of goods sold), Operating Expenses and Net income/Loss
Less sales returns and allowances			
Net sales			
Cost of sales	Year to Date Amount	X	The Cost of Sales/Goods section should show: Beginning inventory, purchases of any goods for sale, and ending inventory.
Beginning inventory			
Plus goods purchased/manufactured			
Total goods available			
Less ending inventory		X	The Operating Expenses section can be broken into Selling Expenses and Geaneral/Administration Expense, this is based on preference.
Total cost of goods sold			
Gross profit (loss)			
Operating Expenses	Year to Date Amount		
Selling			
Salaries and wages			
Commissions			
Advertising			
Depreciation			
Total selling expenses			
General/Administrative			
Salaries and wages			
Employee benefits			
Payroll taxes			
Insurance			
Rent			
Utilities			
Depreciation and amo tization			
Office supplies			
Travel and entertainment			
Postage			
Equipment maintenance and rental			
Interest			
Furniture and equipment			
Total General/Administrative expenses			
Total operating expenses			
Net income before taxes			
Taxes on income			
Net income after taxes			
Extraordinary gain or loss			
Income tax on extraordinary gain			
Net Income (Loss)			

Balance Sheet	Date
ASSETS	Amount
Current Assets	
Cash	
Accounts receivable	
(less doubtful accounts)	
Inventory	
Temporary investment	
Prepaid expenses	
Total Current Assets	
Fixed Assets	
Long-term investments	
Land	
Buildings	
(less accumulated depreciation)	
Plant and equipment	
(less accumulated depreciation)	
Furniture and fixtures	
(less accumulated depreciation)	
Total Net Fixed Assets	
TOTAL ASSETS	
LIABILITIES	Amount
Current Liabilites	
Accounts Payable	
Short Term Notes	
Current Portion of Long Term Notes	
Interest Payable	
Taxes Payable	
Accrued Payroll	
Total Current Liabilities	
Long Term Liabilites	
Mortgage	
Other Long Term Liabilities	
Total Long Term Liabilites	
SHAREHOLDER'S EQUITY	Amount
Capital Stock	
Retained Earnings	
Total Shareholders' Equity	
TOTAL Liabilities and Equity	

Good to know Tips!!

X	The Balance Sheet should include Assets, Liabilites and Shareholder's (Owner's) equity
X	The Asset and Liabilities sections should be broken down into current and long term.
X	Shareholder's Equity should included details based on how the company is organized, whether they have stock shares, one owner, or multiple partners.

STATEMENT OF CASH FLOW

ASSETS	Time Period Amount
Cash flows from operating activities	
Cash received from customers	
Cash paid for merchandise	
Cash paid for wages and other operating expenses	
Cash paid for interest	
Cash paid for taxes	
Other	
Net cash provided (used) by operating activities	
Cash flows from investing activities	
Cash received from sale of capital assets (plant and equipment)	
Cash received from disposition of business segments	
Cash received from collection of notes receivable	
Cash paid for purchase of capital assets	
Cash paid to acquire businesses	
Other	
Net cash provided (used) by investing activities	
Cash flows from financing activities	
Cash received from issuing stock	
Cash received from long-term borro	
Cash paid to repurchase stock	
Cash paid to retire long-term debt	
Cash paid for dividends	
Other	
Net cash provided (used) in financing activities	
Increase (decrease) in cash during the period	
Cash balance at the beginning of the period	
Cash Balance at the end of the period	

Good to know Tips!!

X — The Cash flow should have 3 sections:
Cash from Operating activities
Cash from Investing activities
Cash from financing activities

X — The bottom of the statement should display the beginning balance of cash for the period, the increase or decrease in the balance based on the 3 sections of activities and then the final ending balance.

Investors Notes

CHAPTER 7

TYPES OF ACCOUNTS

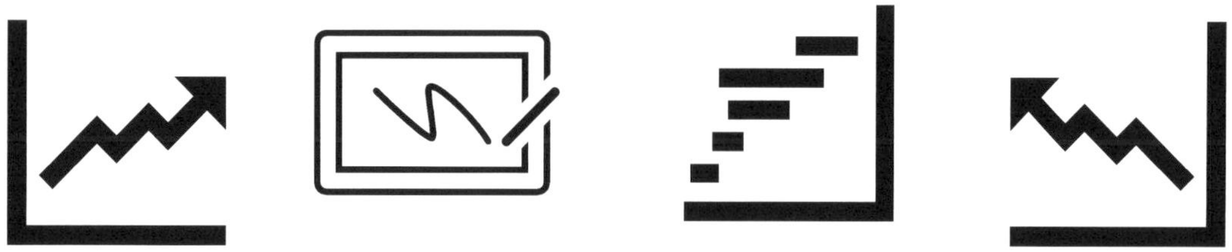

Chapter 7: Types of Accounts

<u>Haggai 1:6</u>
You have planted much, but harvested little… You earn wages, only to put them in a purse with holes in it.

Scripture

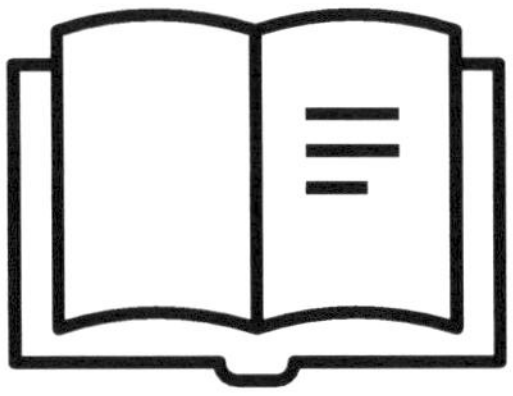

What kind of account should I open?

It's crucial that you keep what you earn in a secure place. When you invest, you need to hold your investments somewhere safe, aka in an account, just like a bank savings or checking account. In this section we'll layout 4 types of investment accounts. Depending on your investment needs and plan, you can decide which will be best for you.

Here are the types of investment accounts.

- Standard Brokerage Account
- Retirement Account
- Education Account
- Custodial Brokerage Account

CHAPTER 7: TYPES OF ACCOUNTS

➢ Standard Brokerage

A standard brokerage account — sometimes called a taxable brokerage account provides you access to a broad range of investments, however, any interest you earn is subject to taxes in the year that the money is received. (ORJ)

➢ Retirement Accounts

A retirement account, such as an IRA, or individual retirement account, it differs from a brokerage account in how the IRS taxes — or doesn't tax —investment gains and withdrawals. (ORJ)

Key Point

A key point of emphasis can be clearly detected in the definition of these two types of accounts. Taxes! Yes, you must be aware of the taxes. There are two categories that any account falls under.

Tax Advantaged Accounts and Non-Tax Advantaged Accounts.

Here's a brief definition of both.

When it comes to "Tax Advantaged Accounts" and "Non-Tax Advantaged Accounts", the thought process is, as we grow our money we want to keep as much of it as we can. Tax advantaged accounts assist us in that, by being tax exempt, tax deferred or having some other significant tax benefit. (INVEST)

Conversely, non-tax advantaged accounts, simply mean you will be taxed. As you identify the type of account best for your situation, you'll want to find out the specific tax implications regarding that account.

Chapter 7: Types of Accounts

Now, it's on to our next accounts.

Education Accounts

An education savings account (ESA) helps you pay for education expenses from grade school to college. (NERD) It is a "Tax Advantaged Account"!

Custodial brokerage accounts

This type of investment account is set up for a minor with money that is gifted to the child. An adult (the custodian) maintains account control and transfers assets to the child when he or she turns the "age of majority," which is either 18 or 21, depending on state laws and or regulations. (NERD)

This type of account is "Non-Tax Advantaged Accounts".

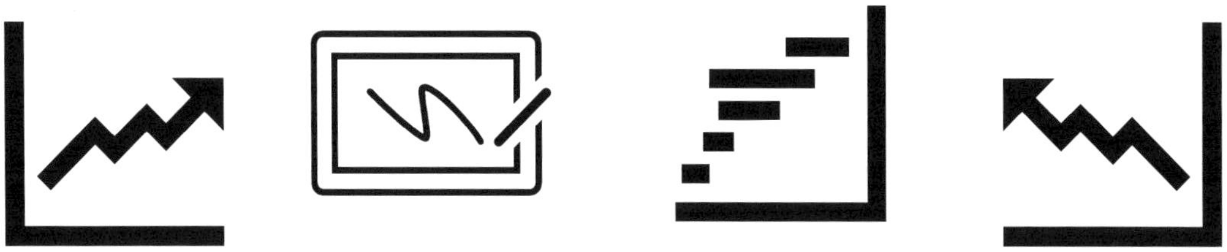

ACTIVITY PAGE

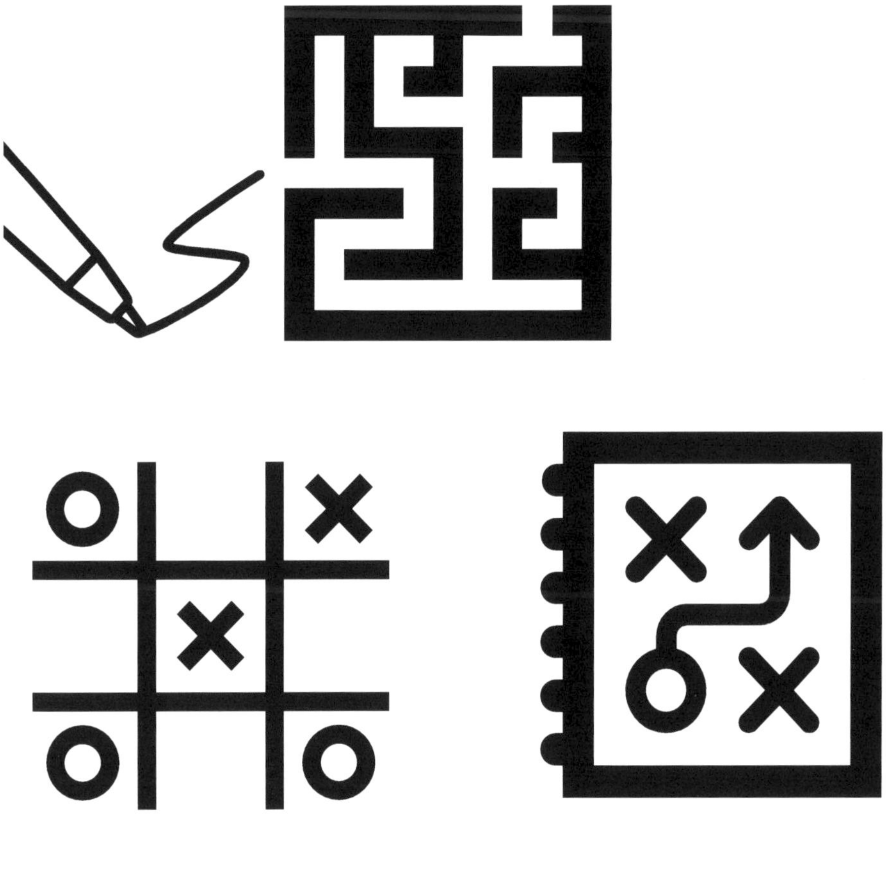

Chapter 7: Activity

Take some time to think about the type of account that's best for you and research the tax implications for that type of account.
Document what you find below.

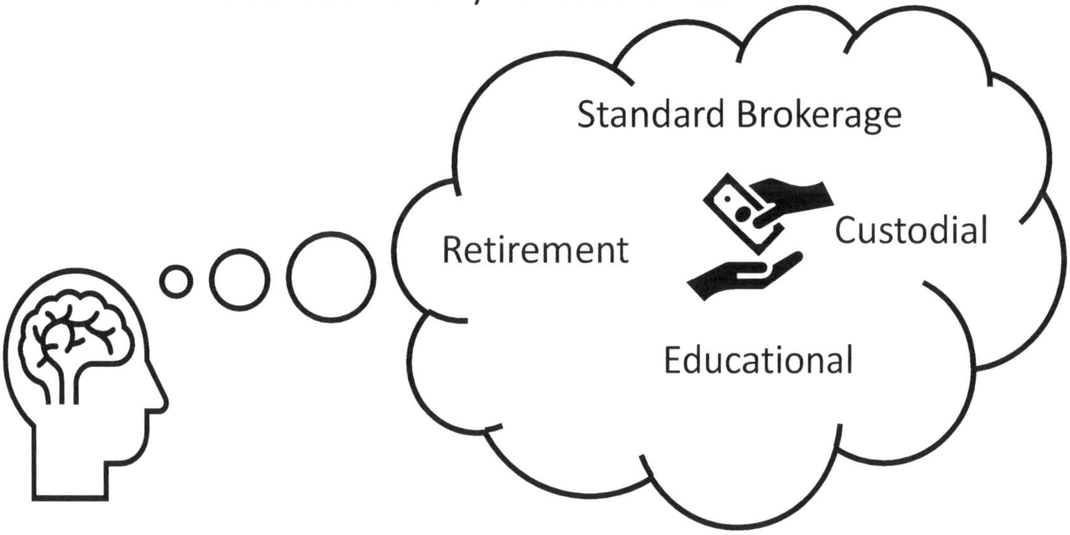

Investors Notes

Chapter 8

Compound Interest:

My how your money can grow $

Chapter 8: Compound Interest

What is Compound Interest?

Compound interest is the interest on a loan or deposit calculated on both the initial amount invested and the added interest on the amount. It is different from simple interest, which is calculated only on the principal amount. It's sometimes called "interest on interest".

Let's simplify these terms a bit. When you were a child did you ever play with Legos or blocks in general? Do you remember trying to stack them up as high as you possibly could? Now imagine you have two identical piles of blocks. With the first pile you set the blocks side by side. This pile is our simple interest pile. With the second pile, instead of spreading them out, you stack the blocks on top of each other one by one. The second pile is our compound interest pile. Now that we have this imagery, let's translate it into numbers.

Side by Side vs Stacked Interest (simple vs compound)

We will now apply our money to our blocks. If you have an investment of $100,000 dollars receiving simple interest at 5% a year, then in ten years you would earn $50,000! Every year you would earn $5,000 ($100,000 x 5%). This is interest being earned separate from any other year's interest. In this way, each year's earnings are set aside from each other. At the end of the ten years, the total amount equals $50,000!

Now, imagine if you had that same $100,000 receiving compound interest at 5% a year over the same ten years you would earn $62,889.46! That's because the $5,000 earned the first year would be stacked on top of or added to, the original $100,000. This means that the second year would be earning 5% on $105,000 not $100,000.

Starting with that second year, every year's earned interest would be added, stacked on top of the growing amount like a mountain of blocks. Your grand total of $62,889.46 would be almost $13,000 more than our simple interest side by side model. This is the power of compounding your money!

Simple Interest			
Year	Principal	Interest	Earnings
1	100000	0.05	5,000.00
2	100000	0.05	5,000.00
3	100000	0.05	5,000.00
4	100000	0.05	5,000.00
5	100000	0.05	5,000.00
6	100000	0.05	5,000.00
7	100000	0.05	5,000.00
8	100000	0.05	5,000.00
9	100000	0.05	5,000.00
10	100000	0.05	5,000.00
			$ 50,000.00

Compound Interest			
Year	Principal	Interest	Earnings
1	100,000.00	0.05	5,000.00
2	105,000.00	0.05	5,250.00
3	110,250.00	0.05	5,512.50
4	115,762.50	0.05	5,788.13
5	121,550.63	0.05	6,077.53
6	127,628.16	0.05	6,381.41
7	134,009.56	0.05	6,700.48
8	140,710.04	0.05	7,035.50
9	147,745.54	0.05	7,387.28
10	155,132.82	0.05	7,756.64
			$ 62,889.46

Activity Page

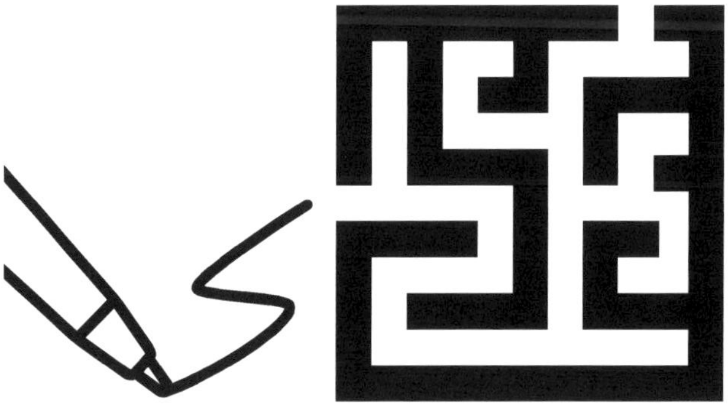

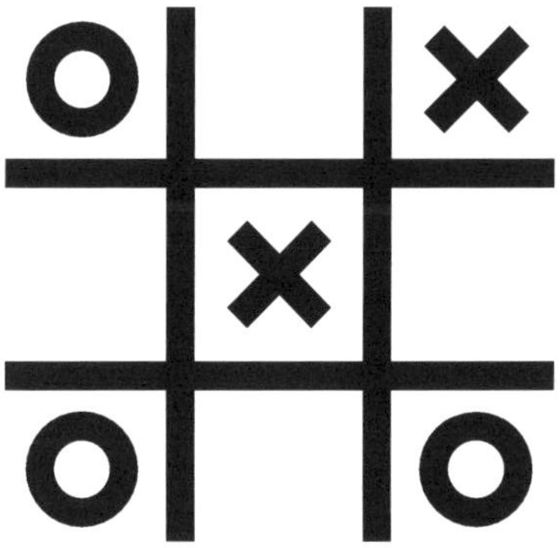

Chapter 8: Activity

One fun way to show the effect of compounding money is to take $.01 and double it for 30 days and see what you produce. This will show you the power of compounding. The first two days have been filled in for you. Continue doubling the amount from the previous day and placing the result in the current day. Repeat until you reach day 30 and see the power of compounding.

Starting Amount	$ 0.01

Day	Amount	Day	Amount
Day 1	$ 0.01	Day 16	
Day 2	$ 0.02	Day 17	
Day 3		Day 18	
Day 4		Day 19	
Day 5		Day 20	
Day 6		Day 21	
Day 7		Day 22	
Day 8		Day 23	
Day 9		Day 24	
Day 10		Day 25	
Day 11		Day 26	
Day 12		Day 27	
Day 13		Day 28	
Day 14		Day 29	
Day 15		Day 30	
		Total after 30 days	

Investors Notes

CHAPTER 9

DEVELOP AN INVESTMENT PLAN

Chapter 9: Develop an Investment Plan

By this point you may feel ready to get going. Well, before you get your feet wet, be sure your plan is solid. I know you may be thinking, "Do I really need an investment plan"? The answer is...Yes!

Habakkuk 2:2
..."Write the vision and make it plain on tablets, that he may run who reads it."

Scripture

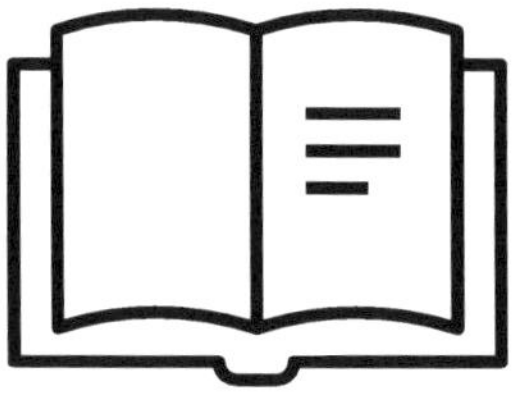

An investment plan puts your investment ideas and strategies into writing and drives you to commit to a disciplined approach. The plan outlines your goals, objectives, and specific tactics that you will use to meet those objectives.

Your investment plan should be for you and your exact situation. It embodies your vision and is the launching pad to get you up and running toward success. So, what are you waiting for, it's time to develop your plan for investing!

Chapter 9: Develop an Investment Plan

Where do you start?

Here are some key steps to get you on the right track.

Step 1: Review your budget from Section 4 and assess your financial position.

Be sure you're able to check off the following.

- Understanding the risks
- Evaluate your Emergency Fund
- Pay off Debt

Step 2: Start with an investment goal.

Your goal should guide the type of investments you make. (ORJ)

Step 3: Investment Idea or Philosophy

Your investment philosophy should include the beliefs and principals that will guide how you invest. (ORJ)

Following these steps will get you off to making a strong investment plan, but what's next...

Setting up your Investment list

After you have your investment plan squared away, proceed to your watchlist! Your watchlist is a list of companies that fit into your investment plan's criteria of good companies to invest in (be sure to note their Ticker Symbol when writing your list, see Glossary for definition). You are literally watching them to see when it's the right time to buy.

Develop your watchlist based on the criteria from section 5. We started with 3 but you can choose any number you're comfortable with. Watch the companies until you identify the right timing and price to invest. When that happens, buy your stock in the company or companies that fit exactly what you're looking for.

Cha-ching! You are now an investor!

ACTIVITY PAGE

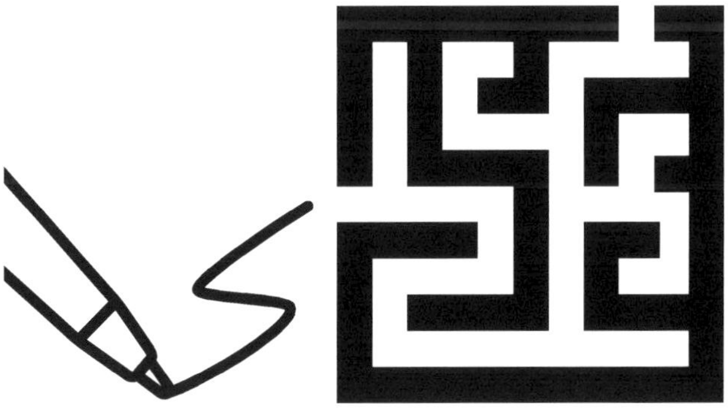

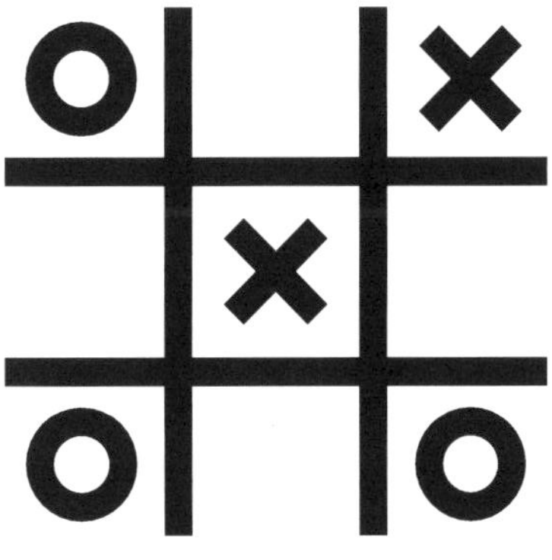

CHAPTER 9: ACTIVITY

Use the below prompts to begin creating your investment plan and then start putting together your watchlist.

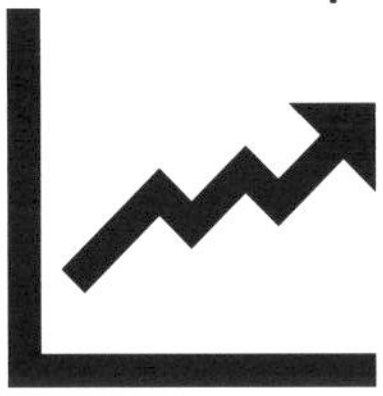

Step 1: Review your budget: Yes/No

- Understanding and document the risks: Yes/No
- Evaluate your Emergency Fund: Yes/No-Amount $__________
- Pay off Debt: Yes/No

Step 2: Investment goal:

____

____

____

Step 3: Investment Idea or Philosophy:

____

____

____

Step 4: Available Funds for Investing: Amount $________________

Step 5: Stock Criteria Checklist:

- Share Price – Amount $______________
- Dividend Payout Yes/No______________
- Profit Margin %_____________________

Investors Notes

CHAPTER 10

MAKING YOUR FIRST INVESTMENT

CHAPTER 10 : MAKING YOUR FIRST INVESTMENT

Here we go! This is the moment you've been waiting for. You've gone through the entire book and now you're ready to make your first investment, but how?

How do you make your first investment?

Here are the steps:

Step 1: Open a Brokerage account with the firm of your choice.

- Three of the top brokerage firms are
  Charles Schwab (www.Schwab.com)
  Fidelity Investment Firm (www.Fidelity.com)
  Vanguard (www.Vanguard.com)
- You will need to provide your personal information in order to open the account. There is usually the option to open a Cash Management Account (which works like a regular bank account) and a Brokerage Account (this is the account you would use to make your actual trades of stock).
- We recommend having both, because having the Cash management account allows you to have money that you are not trading separate from money that you are. It is not required, its just a recommendation.

Step 2: Fund your Account

- Once your account(s) are open you will need to fund the account by linking your new account to an existing bank account.
- After you link the accounts and everything is confirmed, you will then transfer funds into your new Account.

Step 3: Time to Trade

- After funding your account and funds are available, you are now ready to trade. (Note: if you transferred funds into your Cash Management Account, you would now make a transfer to put the desired amount into the Brokerage Account).
- Within your Account, go to the Trade button and type in the Ticker Symbol for the company Stock you want to purchase. Decide if you want to buy in full shares or a specific dollar amount of the stock. Once you have all the info for the order filled in, Execute the order.
- Depending on the firm and type of stock purchased, you will receive a notification from your firm once the order has been fulfilled.

You now own Stock!

Chapter 11

I am an Investor

Chapter 11 : Summary

What have you learned?

Congratulations!!!!! You've made it through this entire workbook! If you followed along, completed all the steps and activities, you have made your first investment and should feel confident in taking the next steps to invest in more good quality stocks.

- You learned some awesome facts about money.
- You learned what investing is and why you should invest.
- You gained valuable insight on generational wealth and the difference between saving and investing.
- You also, have been introduced to stock market terms and history.
- You've built up your investing mentality to be sure you can navigate the ups and downs that occur naturally in the markets.
- You've gone over some of the various types of accounts and even know how to compare simple vs. compounding interest with blocks.
- You've even established your investment plan and developed a watchlist.
- You've opened your investment account and made your very first investment!

- Most importantly, you've got some biblical backup to support everything you've learned and done!!!

Great job! Time to take the show on the road. You got this; you have a starter kit that has prepared you for success.

Just remember, there's much more to learn, discuss and contemplate. However, everyone must start somewhere, and we truly hope that we have helped to get you as ready as can be. Go ahead, take on Wall Street, one stock at a time time.

INVESTORS FINAL THOUGHTS

Crossword Puzzle

Activity

Find all the Investment terms in the following puzzle.

Investment Terms				
Investment	Wealth	Lender	Earnings	Bears
Investor	Portfolio	Borrower	Losses	Money
Stock Market	Gains	Bulls	Market Index	

L	A	D	R	L	H	J	K	B	O	P	T	E	L
O	I	N	V	E	S	T	M	E	N	T	N	A	S
S	N	V	B	N	M	A	X	A	V	N	P	R	Q
S	V	Z	C	D	G	H	E	R	M	X	C	N	T
E	E	B	B	E	N	M	L	S	E	W	Z	I	E
S	S	O	V	R	G	U	E	D	N	U	T	N	K
Q	T	R	F	G	O	X	N	L	P	L	P	G	R
Z	O	R	G	E	C	I	B	G	A	I	N	S	A
X	R	O	C	V	T	U	L	U	D	G	H	L	M
Z	V	W	A	E	N	N	M	O	G	H	D	F	K
F	B	E	K	Y	U	B	O	P	F	T	U	I	C
G	J	R	K	L	C	V	U	Y	W	T	N	M	O
A	A	K	M	N	P	U	T	L	F	H	R	N	T
M	G	M	O	N	E	Y	P	V	L	J	L	O	S
X	W	E	A	L	T	H	N	X	C	S	K	L	P

Glossary Of Terms

Investing Terms

Alpha

This is a term used to describe how much better a portfolio manager, or an investment strategy, performed above the market average. In other words, how much has your investment returned in comparison to the market index.

Beta

Beta measures how sensitive a stock is to the overall movement of the market. In other words, it measures how volatile or risky a stock is compared to the market average.

Appreciation

This is when you see the value of an asset increase over time. For instance, you can say that your home is an appreciating asset if you buy it for $200,000 and then five years later it is worth $250,000.

Depreciation

On the other hand, an asset is depreciating if it loses value over time. For instance, a regular car is a depreciating asset. You buy it for $30,000 brand new and then five years later it is only worth $12,000. Yikes!

Balance sheet

This is a summary of the financial balances of a company. It covers a company's assets, liabilities, and equity at a particular point in time. Basically, it's a snapshot of what a company is worth at that time.

Bear market

You know when someone says, "Man you're acting like a bear," or, "You're a real bear today." Well, this isn't a compliment. It means that you're not being great. This is the same when it comes to the market. When there's a bear market it means the stock market is trending downwards and it's not great.

Bull market

When I think of a bull, I conjure images of a bull charging at me, like in the Pamplona running of the bulls. So, when you put it into the context of the stock market, you can think of a market charging forwards. In other words, a bull market is when things are charging/trending upwards.

Capital

Capital includes cash and other financial assets owned by a person or a company that has value and can give you a future benefit. Examples of capital include cash, stocks, or equipment.

Diversification

This is the process of spreading out your money across several different investments. Diversification is a way to manage risk. Rather than investing all your money in one stock or one company, you can manage your risk by investing across different industries, different sizes of companies (small and large), and even in different countries (emerging markets and developed markets).

Dividend

This is a sum of money that is paid out on a regular basis to shareholders based on the company's earnings. In other words, when the company makes a profit, it shares it with all its shareholders in the form of a dividend. Dividends can be paid out in the form of additional stocks, or in cash.

Emerging market

You see emerging markets in countries where the stock market isn't as developed as the stock market in more developed countries, like the US. An emerging market is found in a country that is transitioning from developing to developed.

Exchange
This is where you go to do your trading. This is where investments are bought and sold. For example, the New York Stock Exchange.

Fiduciary
You might be thinking, what the F is a fiduciary? Great question, let me tell you. When you invest with a financial advisor or a brokerage firm that claims to have a fiduciary responsibility this means they legally must put their clients' best interest ahead of their own. As a fiduciary, they can not mislead you in any way and they must disclose any conflicts of interest. A non-fiduciary advisor or brokerage must invest in a way that is appropriate for their client, but they don't necessarily have to do what is best for their client.

Inflation
You've probably heard of inflation, or even used it in a sentence, "When I was a kid a soda only cost a dollar, thanks a lot inflation!" Inflation is when there is an increase in the price of goods and, as a result, your purchasing power decreases.

P/E ratio
The price to earnings ratio is a way of measuring the value of a company by comparing the price of its stock to its earnings. A P/E ratio can be used by investors to determine if a company's stock is overvalued or undervalued. The P/E ratio tells investors what the market is willing to pay for a specific company today based on it's past or future earnings.

Recession
If you were a young adult during the 2007 to 2009 time period, then you probably remember the last recession. According to the National Bureau of Economic Research, a recession occurs when there is a significant decline in the economy that is spread across the economy and lasts for a span of more than a few months.

Security

A security is a financial asset such as a stock, bond, or option, that can be traded on the stock market.

Shares

Shares are units of ownership in a public company. Shares are bought and sold on the stock market. When you purchase a share in a company you become a shareholder.

Shareholder

When you are a shareholder it means you own one or more shares in a company. When you are a shareholder, you are essentially a part-owner of the company. As a shareholder, you have certain rights including the right to trade your shares on the stock market and the right to share in profitability.

Stock market

The stock market is the place where shares of publicly held companies can be bought and sold. There are many different stock markets around the world, examples include the New York Stock Exchange and the London Stock Exchange. The stock market can also be referred to as a stock exchange.

Ticker (Stock Symbol)

A stock symbol is a unique series of letters assigned to a security for trading purposes. Stocks listed on the New York Stock Exchange (NYSE) can have four or fewer letters. Stock symbols are also known as ticker symbols.

Volatility

Volatility refers to the up and down fluctuations in the market. The more frequently the market swings up and down, the more volatile it is said to be.

Investing strategies

Asset allocation

Asset allocation attempts to balance risk and reward by adjusting the percentage of assets you have invested across different assets (stocks, bonds, cash).

Buy and hold investing

This is an investment strategy where an investor will buy stocks and then hold them for a long period of time ignoring the ups and downs of the market. This is the investment strategy touted by one of the world's most famous investors, Warren Buffet.

Dollar-cost averaging

This is an investment strategy where you invest the same amount of money at regular intervals for an extended period. The goal is to reduce the risk of investing a large sum of money at a "bad time." For instance, if you were to invest your inheritance in the market the day before there was a market crash. Also, dollar-cost averaging can be better for people emotionally. It can be super stressful to invest a huge amount of money – but breaking it up over time it might make it feel more manageable and less scary.

Lump-sum investing

Lump-sum investing is where you take a lump sum of money and invest it all at once.

Investing strategies

Micro investing

This is an investing method that allows you to invest very small amounts of money. Like spare change small. Micro investing is growing in popularity because it's super simple to do. Micro investing also makes investing more accessible because you don't need a huge minimum investment to get started. If you're interested in micro-investing, you can check out the Acorns App. They have a tool called "Round Up" which lets you invest all your spare change from everyday purchases. Maybe you buy a late for $4.50 – the Acorns app will then automatically round up to $5 and invest the $0.50 for you. It makes investing super easy.

Different ways to invest

Stockbroker

This is someone who acts as an intermediary between buyers and sellers of securities (stocks, bonds, etc.). They don't do any investment analysis for you, instead, their job is to execute a buy or sell decision that you've made and then charge you a commission to do so.

Full-service brokerage

This is an institution or firm that assumes the role of intermediary between buyers and sellers of securities. They charge a commission for their services which include financial consulting, money management, and estate planning.

Different ways to invest

Discount brokerage

This is an online trading platform that charges lower fees than a traditional brokerage. Discount brokerages can charge lower fees because they don't offer many of the services provided by a traditional brokerage like investment advice or financial planning. Some examples of popular discount brokerages include E*TRADE and TD Ameritarde. E*TRADE offers a great digital experience with an award-winning app that makes it simple for you to invest from anywhere at any time. They also offer a ton of great content and guidance for new investors to check out. TD Ameritrade is another great option. They offer zero commissions when trading stocks and ETFs, as well as no minimum deposits.

Robo-advisor

A robo-advisor provides investment advice and management using a digital platform. With a robo-advisor, there is little human to human interaction, though if you have a question, you can still speak with a real-live person, not a robot. Rather than having a human investment advisor to do your investing, a robo-advisor uses specialized software and complex algorithms to invest on your behalf. Wealthfront is a popular US robo-advisor that offers several different investment services from retirement investing, and education investing, to investing for any other reason. They offer low fees and can work with you to plan for the future you really want.

Types of investments

Bond

A bond is essentially a loan given to a company or government by investors. Companies and governments borrow money from investors and then pay interest to the investors.

Stock

Often referred to as equity or shares, a stock is a type of investment that represents partial ownership in a company.

Blue-chip investment

You can think of Blue-chip investments as posh investments. They're like the old money of investments. Blue-chip investments refer to the companies that have been around forever, have a long history of good earnings, and a solid balance sheet. They might come off a bit old and boring compared to a new flashy tech company but they're consistent and you can expect good performance from them.

Commodity

A commodity is a raw material that can be bought and sold. Examples of commodities include agricultural (wheat), metals (gold, silver), and energy (oil).

Cryptocurrencies

In the simplest terms, a cryptocurrency is a digital currency that uses cryptography to provide security. Cryptocurrencies are like any other form of currency in that you can use it to make purchases. If you're interested in investing in Cryptocurrencies, you can check out Robinhood. Robinhood Crypto is specifically targeted to investors who are interested in buying and selling cryptocurrencies.

Types of investment funds

ETF

ETF stands for exchange-traded fund. An ETF allows you to purchase many securities – stocks, bonds, or commodities – all at once. You can think of an ETF like a grocery basket but instead of filling your basket with eggs and milk, you fill it with stocks or bonds. And, instead of purchasing each item individually, you purchase the entire basket all in one go! ETFs are traded on an exchange throughout the day and there are tons of ETFs to choose from.

Hedge fund

When you hear the term hedge fund, do you think of rich people? I do. A hedge fund is a pool of money used by investors and institutions who can absorb a loss from a risky trade. Hedge funds are not as regulated as other funds (like a mutual fund) and they also tend to have higher fees. Hedge funds and rich people are often thought of together because it typically requires a large minimum investment to get into a hedge fund.

Index fund

An index fund is a hypothetical portfolio that represents a segment of the financial market. An index fund can be an index mutual fund or an index exchange-traded fund. An example of an index fund is the S&P 500 (a fund that tracks the 500 largest U.S publicly traded companies). There are all kinds of index funds, ones for metals, ones for the tech sector, ones for bonds, you can find an index fund for almost anything.

Types of investment funds

Mutual fund

A mutual fund is a professionally managed investment fund that pools money from investors to purchase different investments (stocks, bonds, etc). By pooling your investments with others, you're able to invest in a much wider mix of investments than you would likely be able to afford on your own. Mutual funds are managed by a fund manager who decides when to buy and sell investments depending on the type of fund.

REITs

REITs, or real estate investment trusts, are companies that own or finance income-producing real estate across a range of property sectors.

Retirement investing terms

Traditional IRA

A traditional IRA is an individual retirement account that offers tax advantages when you save for your retirement. A traditional IRA is tax-deductible. This means that the contributions you make to your traditional IRA will help to lower your taxable income. With a traditional IRA, you pay taxes when you start to withdraw your money.

401(k)

This is a common retirement savings account offered by many employers. With a 401(k) you can contribute a specified amount and this amount will be deducted from your taxable income. So, if you make $100,000 per year and contribute $10,000 to your 401(k), then you will only be taxed on $90,000 income.

Roth IRA

A Roth IRA is an individual retirement account that offers tax advantages including tax-free growth on your investments and tax-free withdrawals in retirement. A Roth IRA is funded with post-tax money, meaning money you've already paid your taxes on. For help with retirement investing, you can check out Betterment, offering personalized advice that can help you make the most from your Roth IRA (or Traditional or SEP IRA). If you have no clue as to which type of IRA to open, you can start by using Betterment's easy-to-use guidance that can walk you through which account is right for your future retirement needs. Betterment will also help you create an entire retirement plan that you can access from your account, where you map out your goals and how much you'd like to save. And Betterment automatically rebalances your portfolio to align with your goals.

Investment Account Types

A standard brokerage account

sometimes called a taxable brokerage account provides you access to a broad range of investments, however, any interest you earn is subject to taxes in the year that the money is received.

Retirement Accounts

A retirement account, such as an IRA, or individual retirement account, it differs from a brokerage account in how the IRS taxes — or doesn't tax — investment gains and withdrawals.

Education Accounts

An education savings account (ESA) helps you pay for education expenses from throughout grade school to college.

Custodial brokerage accounts

This type of investment account is set up for a minor with money that is gifted to the child. An adult (the custodian) maintains account control and transfers assets to the child when he or she turns the "age of majority," which is either 18 or 21, depending on state laws and or regulations.

Additional Terms

Credit

The ability to borrow money or access goods or services with the understanding that you'll pay later.

Credibility

The level of which your credit is measured.

Debtor

is a company or individual who owes money. If the debt is in the form of a loan from a financial institution, the debtor is referred to as a borrower, and if the debt is in the form of securities—such as bonds—the debtor is referred to as an issuer.

Generational wealth

Generational wealth refers to resources passed on from one generation of a family to another, such as stocks, bonds, real estate, and family businesses.

Lender

is an individual, a public or private group, or a financial institution that makes funds available to a person or business with the expectation that the funds will be repaid. Repayment will include the payment of any interest or fees.

Market Index

A stock market index is an index or guide that measures a stock market, or a subset of the stock market, that helps investors compare current price levels with past prices to calculate market performance.

Portfolio

A portfolio is a collection of financial investments like stocks, bonds, commodities etc.

S&P 500

The Standard & Poor's 500 measures the value of the stocks of the 500 largest corporations by market capitalization

Reference for all Terms

All terms in the glossary are referenced from the following sources.

https://www.merriam-webster.com

https://www.moneyunder30.com

https://www.nerdwallet.com/article/investing/types-investment-accounts-know

https://Investopedia.com

Need more budget & tax support?
We can help.

Click below!

- Budget and Finance: Financial Planning, Organizing & Accounting Resource Series:

https://amzn.to/3gEiMuu

Also, Check out our entire resource library, link below!

- All Kingdom Khai Resources:

https://bit.ly/kingdom_resources

SCRIPTURES

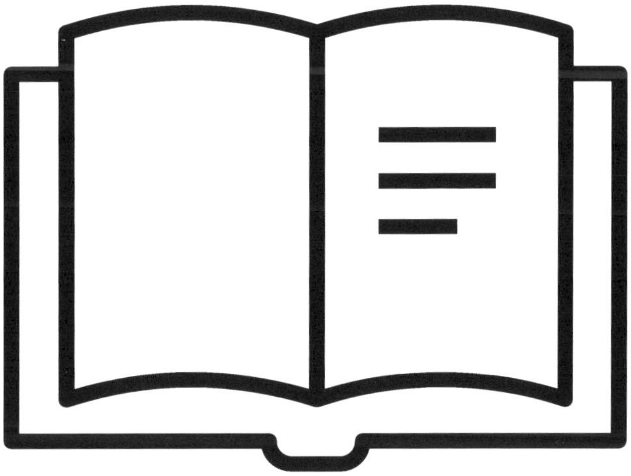

Scriptures

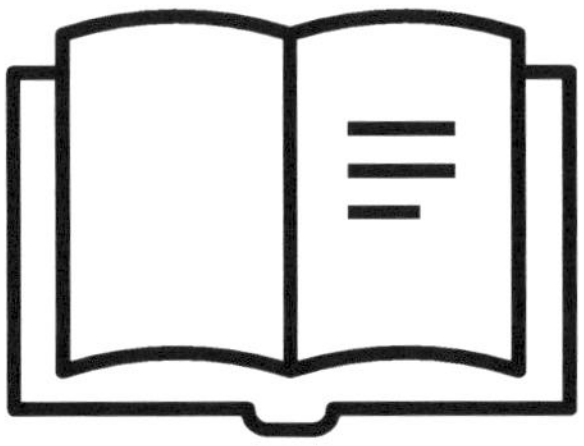

- ***Proverbs 13:22:*** "A good man leaves an inheritance to his children's children."

- ***Ecclesiastes 5:10*** Whoever loves money never has enough; whoever loves wealth is never satisfied with their income. This too is meaningless.

- ***Matthew 25:14–18*** "Again, it will be like a man going on a journey, who called his servants and entrusted his wealth to them. 15 To one he gave five bags of gold, to another two bags, and to another one bag,[a] each according to his ability. Then he went on his journey. 16 The man who had received five bags of gold went at once and put his money to work and gained five bags more. 17 So also, the one with two bags of gold gained two more. 18 But the man who had received one bag went off, dug a hole in the ground and hid his master's money…

- ***Proverbs: 22:7*** The rich rule over the poor and the borrower is slave to the lender.

- ***Haggai 1:6*** You have planted much, but harvested little… You put on clothes but are not warm. You earn wages, only to put them in a purse with holes in it.

Scriptures

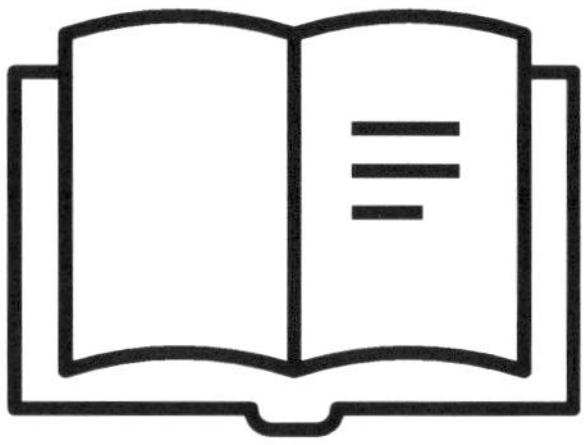

- **Matthew 6:33** But seek ye first the kingdom of God, and his righteousness; and all these things shall be added unto you.

- **Ecclesiastes 5:10** Whoever loves money never has enough; whoever loves wealth is never satisfied with their income. This too is meaningless.
- **Romans 8:28** All things work together for good to them that love God, to them who are the called according to his purpose.

- **Philippians 4:8** Finally, brethren, whatsoever things are true, whatsoever things are honest, whatsoever things are just, whatsoever things are pure, whatsoever things are lovely, whatsoever things are of good report; if there be any virtue, and if there be any praise, think on these things.

- **Luke 14:28-30** If you wanted to build a tower, you would first sit down and decide how much it would cost. You must see if you have enough money to finish the job. If you don't do that, you might begin the work, but you would not be able to finish. And if you could not finish it, then all who would see it would laugh at you. They would say, 'This man began to build but was not able to finish!

- **Matthew 6:21** For where your treasure is, there will your heart be also.

Scriptures Affirmations

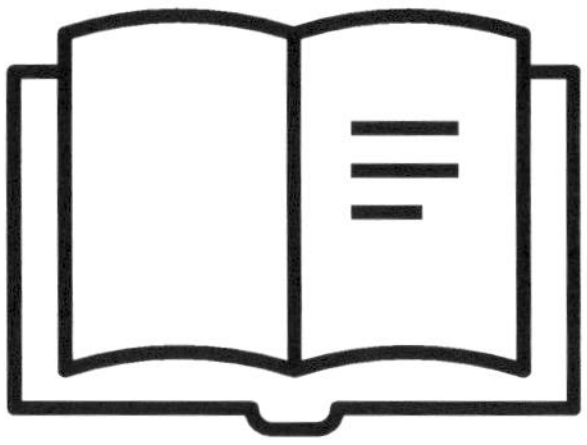

- **I am a beloved child of the Most High Creator.** *(Jeremiah 31:3)*
- **I am held in my Father's hand and need not fear.** *(John 10:28-29)*
- **I am worthy of love because God loves me.** *(Ephesians 2:4-5)*
- **I am treasured by the Father.** *(Deuteronomy 14:2)*
- **I am God's masterpiece.** *(Ephesians 2:10)*
- **I am chosen and appointed by God.** *(John 15:16)*
- **I am healed from sin by God's love.** *(1 Peter 2:24)*
- **I am abundant.** *(2 Corinthians 12:9)*
- **I am fearfully and wonderfully made.** *(Psalm 139:14)*
- **I am brave.** *(Psalm 23:4)*
- **I am made in the image of God.** *(Genesis 1:27)*
- **I am free.** *(Galatians 5:1)*
- **I am redeemed through the Messiah.** *(Ephesians 1:7)*
- **I am triumphant.** *(1 John 5:4)*
- **I am gifted.** *(1 Peter 4:10)*

Answer Keys

KEY

Investment Terms				
Investment	Wealth	Lender	Earnings	Bears
Investor	Portfolio	Borrower	Losses	Money
Stock Market	Gains	Bulls	Market Index	

L				L				B				E	
O	I	N	V	E	S	T	M	E	N	T		A	
S	N			N				A				R	
S	V			D				R		X		N	T
E	E	B		E				S	E			I	E
S	S	O		R				D				N	K
	T	R			O		N					G	R
	O	R				I		G	A	I	N	S	A
	R	O			T		L						M
		W		E				O					K
		E	K			B			F				C
		R					U			T			O
	A							L			R		T
M		M	O	N	E	Y			L			O	S
	W	E	A	L	T	H				S			P

Activity: Compound Interest

KEY

Starting Amount	$ 0.01		
Day	**Amount**	**Day**	**Amount**
Day 1	$ 0.01	Day 16	$ 327.68
Day 2	$ 0.02	Day 17	$ 655.36
Day 3	$ 0.04	Day 18	$ 1,310.72
Day 4	$ 0.08	Day 19	$ 2,621.44
Day 5	$ 0.16	Day 20	$ 5,242.88
Day 6	$ 0.32	Day 21	$ 10,485.76
Day 7	$ 0.64	Day 22	$ 20,971.52
Day 8	$ 1.28	Day 23	$ 41,943.04
Day 9	$ 2.56	Day 24	$ 83,886.08
Day 10	$ 5.12	Day 25	$ 167,772.16
Day 11	$ 10.24	Day 26	$ 335,544.32
Day 12	$ 20.48	Day 27	$ 671,088.64
Day 13	$ 40.96	Day 28	$ 1,342,177.28
Day 14	$ 81.92	Day 29	$ 2,684,354.56
Day 15	$ 163.84	Day 30	$ 5,368,709.12
		Total after 30 days	$ 5,368,709.12

References

https://shorelinecu.org/hometown-rewards/the-hometown-kids-club/fun-money-facts/

https://www.money254.co.ke/post/the-7-types-of-personal-budgets-and-how-to-choose-money-management (MONEY254)

https://www.clevergirlfinance.com/blog/money-facts/

https://www.easypeasyfinance.com/budget-for-kids-beginners-budgeting/

https://www.webmd.com/mental-health/positive-thinking-overview (WEBMD)

https://greatist.com/live/how-to-stay-positive-around-negative-people

https://bydeze.com/christian-affirmations/

https://corporatefinanceinstitute.com/resources/accounting/types-of-budgets-budgeting-methods/U (CORP)

https://www.thepennyhoarder.com/budgeting/simple-budget/

https://www.psychologytoday.com/us/blog/fixing-families/201410/whats-your-state-mind (Psychologytoday)

https://ourrichjourney.thinkific.com/courses/InvestingforFIRE (ORJ)

https://www.investopedia.com/ (INVEST)

https://www.biblegateway.com/

https://www.ramseysolutions.com/financial-literacy/teaching-compound-interest (RAMSEY)

https://www.techtarget.com/searchwindowsserver/definition/system (TECH)

https://www.merriam-webster.com (WEBSTER)

https://www.moneyunder30.com

https://www.nerdwallet.com/article/investing/types-investment-accounts-know (NERD)

If you enjoyed your

HOW TO INVEST
FOR BEGINNERS BOOK

Please leave us a review!

Reviews will help us continue to make more wonderful journals
like this one for you and others.

Kingdom Khai
Cultivating World Class Kingdom Resources ™

Published by Kingdom Khai, LLC.
www.KingdomKhai.com

Made in the USA
Monee, IL
24 November 2024

71101477R00081